COUNTRY COOKING
RECIPES FROM WALES

COGINIO GWLEDIG - RYSEITIAU O GYMRU

Sian Llewellyn

DOMINO BOOKS (WALES) LTD

METRIC/IMPERIAL/AMERICAN UNITS

We are all used to doubling or halving a recipe. Thus, a Victoria sandwich may be made using 4 oz each of flour, sugar and butter with 2 eggs or 6 oz each of flour, sugar and butter with 3 eggs. The proportions of the ingredients are unchanged. This must be so for all units. Use either the metric units or the imperial units given in the recipes, do not mix the two.

It is not practical to give the exact equivalents of metric and imperial units because 1 oz equals 28.35 g and 1 pint equals 568 ml. The tables on page vi indicate suitable quantities but liquids should be carefully added to obtain the correct consistency. See also the charts on page iv.

PINTS TO MILLILITRES AND LITRES
The following are approximations only

$\frac{1}{4}$ pint = 150 ml

$\frac{1}{2}$ pint = 275 ml

$\frac{3}{4}$ pint = 425 ml

1 pint = 575 ml

$1\frac{3}{4}$ pints = 1000 ml (1 litre)

3 pints = $1\frac{1}{2}$ litres

CONTENTS - CYNNWYS

Page - Tudalen

© D C P and E J P. This edition printed 2012
Welsh translation by Delyth Evans - Cyfieithiad Cymraeg gan Delyth Evans
Cover photograph by Jonathan Tew - Llun y clawr gan Jonathan Tew
Illustrations by Allison Fewtrell - Darluniau gan Allison Fewtrell
ISBN 978 1 85772 008 2
Typeset by Domino Books (Wales) Ltd

Domino Books (Wales) Ltd
P O Box 32
Swansea SA1 1FN
UK
Tel. 01792 459378
email: sales@dominobooks.co.uk
www.dominobooks.co.uk

The following charts give the approximate equivalents for metric and imperial weights, and oven temperatures.

Ounces	Approx g to nearest whole number	Approx g to nearest whole 25 g
1	28	25
2	57	50
3	85	75
4	113	125
5	142	150
6	170	175
7	198	200
8	226	225
9	255	250
10	283	275
11	311	300
12	340	350
13	368	375
14	396	400
15	428	425
16	456	450

OVEN TEMPERATURE GUIDE

	Electricity °C	°F	Gas Mark
Very cool	110	225	$\frac{1}{4}$
	130	250	$\frac{1}{2}$
Cool	140	275	1
	150	300	2
Moderate	170	325	3
	180	350	4
Moderately hot	190	375	5
	200	400	6
Hot	220	425	7
	230	450	8
Very hot	240	475	9

When using this chart for weights over 16 ounces, add the appropriate figures in the column giving the nearest whole number of grammes and then adjust to the nearest unit of 25. For example, 18 oz (16 oz + 2 oz) becomes 456 + 57 = 513 to the nearest whole number and 525 g to the nearest unit of 25.

Throughout the book, 1 teaspoon = 5 ml and 1 tablespoon = 15 ml.

FOREWORD - RHAGAIR

When the only mode of transport was the horse and most journeys took several days, housewives were expected to provide a meal for any unexpected guests. Visitors were valued for their company and for the news they brought with them.

Much of Welsh cooking grew out of the need to provide a diet from frugal resources that could sustain the farmworker and miner. At the turn of the century, the diet was based mainly on root vegetables and cereals with a little meat, mainly pork. A typical Welsh soup, *cawl,* was made from scraps of bacon, lamb, cabbage, swede, new potatoes and leeks with sometimes a wood pigeon and cheese.

Food was cooked in a pot suspended over the fire in the kitchen or on a flat bakestone. On this griddle, pancakes, Welsh cakes, teisen lap, caraway cake and honey cake were baked.

Much of Wales is close to the sea with a ready supply of mackerel, herring and sea trout. The Principality is rich in rivers with salmon and trout there for the taking. Trout was often wrapped in bacon or greased lightly with bacon fat and wrapped in the leaves of a leek. Salmon requires the more subtle touch of a light sauce. From the Gower came laverbread, from Porteynon oysters, and from Penclawdd cockles. And all of this delicious, wholesome fare can be bought today at any Welsh market.

Some of the recipes for these are in this book, others are in the companion books, *The Welsh Pantry, Welsh Kitchen* and *Celtic Recipes.* In some instances, they have been modified slightly to suit the more sedentary lifestyles of today but they still retain their nutritional value and their special Welsh flavour.

S L

AMERICAN MEASURES

American measures are given by volume and weight using standard cups and spoons.

US Standard Measuring Spoons and Cups

1 tablespoon = 3 teaspoons = $\frac{1}{2}$ fluid ounce = 14•2 ml
2 tablespoons = 1 fluid ounce $\doteq$ 28 ml
4 tablespoons = $\frac{1}{4}$ cup
5 tablespoons = $\frac{1}{3}$ cup
8 tablespoons = $\frac{1}{2}$ cup
10 tablespoons = $\frac{2}{3}$ cup
12 tablespoons = $\frac{3}{4}$ cup
16 tablespoons = 1 cup = 8 fluid ounces = $\frac{1}{2}$ US pint
32 tablespoons = 2 cups = 16 fluid ounces = 1 US pint.

Metric (Imperial)	American
1 teaspoon	1 teaspoon
1 tablespoon	1 tablespoon
$1\frac{1}{2}$ tablespoons	2 tablespoons
2 tablespoons	3 tablespoons
3 tablespoons	$\frac{1}{4}$ (scant) cup
4 tablespoons	5 tablespoons
5 tablespoons	6 tablespoons
$5\frac{1}{2}$ tablespoons	7 tablespoons
6 tablespoons (scant $\frac{1}{4}$ pint)	$\frac{1}{2}$ cup
$\frac{1}{4}$ pint	$\frac{2}{3}$ cup
scant $\frac{1}{2}$ pint	1 cup
$\frac{1}{2}$ pint (10 fl oz)	$1\frac{1}{4}$ cups
$\frac{3}{4}$ pint (15 fl oz)	scant 2 cups
$\frac{4}{5}$ pint (16 fl oz)	2 cups (1 pint)
1 pint (20 fl oz)	$2\frac{1}{2}$ cups

Metric (Imperial)	American
flour, plain or self-raising	
15 g ($\frac{1}{2}$ oz)	2 tablespoons
25 g (1oz)	$1\frac{1}{4}$ cups
100/125 g (4 oz)	1 cup
sugar, caster or granulated, brown (firmly packed)	
25 g (1 oz)	2 tablespoons
100/125 g (4 oz)	$\frac{1}{2}$ cup
200/225 g (8 oz)	1 cup
butter, margarine, fat	
1 oz	2 tablespoons
225 g (8 oz)	1 cup
150 g (5 oz) shredded suet	1 cup

1 cup (American) contains approximately

100/125 g (4 oz) grated cheese, 50 g (2 oz) fresh breadcrumbs,
100 g (4 oz) dried breadcrumbs,
100/125 g (4 oz) pickled beetroot, button mushrooms, shelled peas, red/blackcurrants, 5 oz strawberries,
175 g (6 oz) raisins, currants, sultanas, chopped candied peel, stoned dates,
225 g (8 oz) glace cherries, 150 g (5 oz) shelled whole walnuts,
100 g (4 oz) chopped nuts,
75 g (3 oz) desiccated coconut,
225 g (8 oz) cottage cheese,
100/125 g (4 oz) curry powder,
225 g (8 oz) minced raw meat,
$\frac{3}{8}$ pint ($7\frac{1}{2}$ fl oz) cream.

SOUPS - CAWL

HARVEST BROTH - CAWL CYNHAEAF

METRIC
1 kg Welsh neck of lamb
200 g peas
200 g broad beans
1 medium sized carrot
1 onion
1 small turnip
1 small cauliflower
5 sprigs parsley
1.5 litres water
salt and pepper

IMPERIAL
2 lb Welsh neck of lamb
8 oz peas
8 oz broad beans
1 medium sized carrot
1 onion
1 small turnip
1 small cauliflower
5 sprigs parsley
3 pints water
salt and pepper

Remove as much fat as possible from the meat. Place the meat in a large saucepan and cover with the water. Bring to the boil and skim any fat from the surface of the liquid. Shell the peas and beans. Peel and dice the carrot, onion and turnip. Add the vegetables, except the cauliflower, to the meat. Season. Cover the saucepan and simmer slowly for 3 hours. 30 minutes before serving the broth, cut the cauliflower into sprigs and add to the saucepan. Serve hot decorated with sprigs of parsley.

MICHAELMAS BROTH - POTES GŴYL MIHANGEL

METRIC
*1 small chicken
2 litres water
1 onion, diced
50 g carrot, diced
50 g celery, cut up
2 tablespoons long grain rice
salt and pepper

IMPERIAL
*1 small chicken
4 pints water
1 onion, diced
2 oz carrot, diced
2 oz celery, cut up
2 tablespoons long grain rice
salt and pepper

Clean the chicken and cut into joints. Place in a large pan with the onion, carrot and celery. Season. Bring to the boil. Cover and simmer for 3 hours. Skim any fat from the surface of the liquid from time to time. Remove the chicken and strain the broth. Return the broth to the pan and sprinkle in the rice. Simmer for 15 - 20 minutes. Serve the broth hot alone or with some of the chicken, finely chopped. The chicken can be used in other dishes.

Traditonally, goose was used and the cawl thickened with oatmeal. Today, goose is considered to be too fatty. A chicken or turkey carcass can be used instead of a whole bird.

BACON SOUP - CAWL CIG MOCH

METRIC
150 g lean bacon rashers
1 medium sized potato
2 leeks
1 stalk celery
1 egg

IMPERIAL
6 oz lean bacon rashers
1 medium sized potato
2 leeks
1 stalk celery
1 egg

METRIC	**IMPERIAL**
600 ml water	*1 pint water*
600 ml milk	*1 pint milk*
2 teaspoons chopped parsley	*2 teaspoons chopped parsley*
salt and pepper	*salt and pepper*

Remove the rind from the bacon. Dice the bacon. Peel and cut up the potato and leeks. Slice the celery. Place the bacon and vegetables with the water in a saucepan. Season. Cover and simmer for 30 minutes. Separate the egg yolk from the white and mix the yolk with the milk. Remove the saucepan from the heat and stir in the egg yolk and milk. Reheat for 2 - 3 minutes but do not boil. Serve sprinkled with parsley.

TOMATO AND APPLE SOUP - CAWL TOMATO AC AFAL

METRIC	**IMPERIAL**
450 g tomatoes	*1 lb tomatoes*
225 g onions	*8 oz onions*
450 g cooking apples	*1 lb cooking apples*
600 ml chicken stock	*1 pint chicken stock*
salt and pepper	*salt and pepper*
chives for garnish	*chives for garnish*
cream	*cream*

Place the tomatoes in boiling water for 2 - 3 minutes then in cold water. The skins will now peel off easily. Cut up the tomatoes. Peel and cut up the onions and apples. Place the tomatoes, onions and apples with the stock in a saucepan. Season. Bring to the boil and simmer for 20 minutes until the onions are soft. Purée the mixture and then sieve to remove the tomato pips. The soup should be completely smooth. Serve hot, garnished with chives and cream or chilled.

BEEF BROTH - POTES CIG EIDION

METRIC
1 kg stewing beef
200 g carrots
1 small swede
200 g potatoes
2 leeks
1 small cabbage
1 tablespoon flour
salt and pepper
parsley

IMPERIAL
2 lb stewing beef
8 oz carrots
1 small swede
8 oz potatoes
2 leeks
1 small cabbage
1 tablespoon flour
salt and pepper
parsley

Cut the meat into 2.5 cm (1 inch) cubes and remove any fat. Season and cook in 1 litre (2 pints) of water for 15 minutes. Peel and cut up the carrots, swede and potatoes. Wash and cut up the leeks. Shred the leaves of the cabbage. Add the vegetables to the meat, adjust seasoning and cook for 20 minutes. Make a smooth paste with the flour and a little of the broth and work in. Stir the flour paste into the broth and warm to thicken. Serve hot garnished with parsley.

DUMPLINGS FOR SOUP - DWMPLINS AR GYFER CAWL

METRIC
100 g self raising flour
50 g shredded suet
salt and pepper

IMPERIAL
4 oz self raising flour
2 oz shredded suet
salt and pepper

Mix the flour and suet together. Season. Bind to an elastic dough with a little water. Separate into small balls and roll lightly in flour. Add to the soup about 15 - 20 minutes before it is to be served. (These are filling and turn almost any soup into a meal. If preferred, grated onion and a little mixed herbs may be mixed into the flour.)

SAVOURY DISHES - BLASUSFWYD

ANGLESEY EGGS - WYAU SIR FÔN

METRIC
450 g potatoes
3 leeks
4 eggs
Sauce
50 g butter
50 g flour
600 ml milk
75 g Caerphilly cheese
salt and pepper

IMPERIAL
1 lb potatoes
3 leeks
4 eggs
Sauce
2 oz butter
2 oz flour
1 pint milk
3 oz Caerphilly cheese
salt and pepper.

Boil the eggs hard and shell. Peel and boil the potatoes in salted water. Wash and cut up the leeks. Boil the leeks for 10 minutes in salted water until soft. Drain the potatoes and leeks and mash together. Season.

Sauce: Melt the butter in a saucepan. Remove from the heat and add the flour. Work to a smooth paste. Stir in the milk, keeping the mixture free from lumps. Heat gently, stirring all the time, until the mixture thickens. Cook gently for 2 - 3 minutes. Grate the cheese and stir half into the sauce. Cut the eggs in half and place in an ovenproof dish. Place or pipe the potato and leek mixture around the eggs, pour over the sauce and sprinkle with the remaining cheese. Heat under the grill or in the oven until golden brown. (If preferred, serve in individual dishes.)

CHEESE AND POTATO EGGS - WYAU GYDA CAWS A THATWS

METRIC	IMPERIAL
400 g potatoes	1 lb potatoes
100 g cheese	4 oz cheese
25 g butter	1 oz butter
1 tablespoon chopped chives	1 tablespoon chopped chives
4 tablespoons breadcrumbs	4 tablespoons breadcrumbs
4 eggs	4 eggs
salt and pepper	salt and pepper
2 tablespoons milk	2 tablespoons milk
fat for frying	fat for frying

Boil the eggs hard and shell. Peel and cut up the potatoes and cook in salted water. Grate the cheese. Mix the potatoes with the cheese, chives and butter. Season. Divide and form into 4 rounds. Place an egg on each round and the cheese and potato mixture round the eggs. Brush with milk and coat with breadcrumbs. Fry in deep fat until golden. Drain on kitchen paper.

CAERPHILLY PUDDING - PWDIN CAERFFILI

METRIC	IMPERIAL
50 g Caerphilly cheese	2 oz Caerphilly cheese
50 g breadcrumbs	2 oz breadcrumbs
25 g butter	1 oz butter
300 ml milk	$\frac{1}{2}$ pint milk
2 eggs	2 eggs
pinch of salt	pinch of salt

Grate the cheese. Mix half the cheese with the breadcrumbs. Add the salt. Warm the milk and butter until the butter melts. Pour over the cheese mixture. Separate the yolks and whites of the eggs. Lightly beat the yolks and stir into the cheese mixture. Bake in a moderate oven (170°C, 325°F, gas mark 3) for 30 minutes. Beat the egg whites until stiff and spread over the pudding. Sprinkle with the remaining cheese and return to the oven until brown.

LEEK AND SHERRY CASSEROLE - CASSEROLE CENNIN A SIERI

METRIC	IMPERIAL
4 leeks	*4 leeks*
2 rashers Welsh bacon	*2 rashers Welsh bacon*
1 carrot	*1 carrot*
1 celery stalk	*1 celery stalk*
25 g butter	*1 oz butter*
3 tablespoons sherry	*3 tablespoons sherry*
150 ml milk	*$\frac{1}{4}$ pint milk*
3 tablespoons cream	*3 tablespoons cream*
pinch of salt and dried sage	*pinch of salt and dried sage*

Wash and cut up the celery stalk. Peel and slice the carrot. Remove the rind and dice the bacon. Place the vegetables and bacon in a pan with the butter and fry until softened. Wash and slice the leeks lengthwise. Place in the bottom of a greased ovenproof dish and cover with the bacon and the other vegetables. Add the seasoning, sherry and milk. Cover and cook in a moderate oven (180°C, 350°F, gas mark 4) for 45 minutes. Serve hot with a little cream.

THE MISER'S FEAST - GWLEDD Y CYBYDD

METRIC
1 kg potatoes
200 g onions
25 g butter
10 Welsh bacon rashers
salt and pepper

IMPERIAL
2 lb potatoes
8 oz onions
1 oz butter
10 Welsh bacon rashers
salt and pepper

Peel and slice the potatoes and onions. Boil in salted water. Drain and mash with the butter. Add pepper to taste and place in an ovenproof dish. Remove the rind and fat from the bacon rashers and place on top of the potato and onion mixture. Heat in a moderate oven (180°C, 350°F, gas mark 4) until the bacon is crisp.

LEEK AND POTATO PIE - PASTAI CENNIN A THATWS

Use 2 leeks washed and cut up finely instead of onions in the above recipe.

LAVERBREAD AND FRIED BREAD - BARA LAWR A BARA WEDI FFRIO

METRIC
*450 g prepared laverbread
8 rashers of Welsh bacon
4 slices of bread
bacon fat for frying

IMPERIAL
*1 lb prepared laverbread
8 rashers of Welsh bacon
4 slices of bread
bacon fat for frying

Cook the bacon, remove from the pan and keep warm. Fry the slices of bread until crisp. Place with the bacon. Using a spoon, form the laverbread into 4 cakes and cook in the bacon fat for 4 - 5 minutes until thoroughly cooked through. Serve hot with the laverbread on top of the bread and covered with the bacon rashers.

*The laverbread bought in the shops and markets has already been washed and boiled for several hours. It is ready for frying and is sold with or without oatmeal. The flavour of laverbread is enhanced if it is chilled in the refrigerator for an hour or so before being cooked.

SEAFOOD PANCAKES - CREMPOG BWYD Y MÔR

METRIC
Batter
100 g plain flour
250 ml milk
1 egg
pinch of salt
fat for frying
Filling
300 g peeled, cooked prawns

IMPERIAL
Batter
4 oz plain flour
½ pint milk
1 egg
pinch of salt
fat for frying
Filling
12 oz peeled, cooked prawns

Sift the flour and salt into a mixing bowl. Make a well in the middle and break the egg into this. Add the milk a little at a time and work into a smooth batter. Beat well and leave to stand for 30 minutes. Brush the frying pan with a little fat and heat until fairly hot. Pour just enough batter into the pan to cover the bottom thinly. When cooked on one side, turn and cook on the other side. Place on a plate and keep warm. Repeat until the batter is used up. To serve, place prawns in the centre of each pancake and roll up.

Other fillings include cooked flaked fish, cockles (cooked and drained) and smoked salmon.

CHEESY PANCAKES - CREMPOG CAWS

Make pancakes as for seafood pancakes. Mix grated Caerphilly cheese with cream. Season. Place a little of the mixture on each pancake and roll up. Serve hot.

LEEKS AND PANCAKES - CENNIN A CHREMPOG

Make pancakes as for seafood pancakes. Wash and cut up 2 leeks. Fry with 125 g (6 oz) button mushrooms in 25 gm (1 oz) butter. Season. Place a little of the leek and mushroom mixture in the middle of each pancake and roll up. Serve hot.

HAM OMELETTE - OMLET HAM

METRIC	IMPERIAL
2 eggs	2 eggs
25 g cooked ham, chopped	1 oz cooked ham, chopped
1 tablespoon water	1 tablespoon water
salt and pepper	salt and pepper
nub butter	nub butter

Lightly whisk the eggs. Season with salt and pepper and add the water. Stir in the chopped meat. Heat a pan and grease lightly with the butter. When hot, pour in the eggs. Stir until the eggs set then allow to cook for 1 minute until the omelette is golden brown underneath but still creamy and soft on the top. Tilting the pan, fold the omelette in half and serve hot.

SAVOURY OMELETTES - OMLETAU SAFRI

Omit the ham from the recipe for savoury omelette. Cook 50 g (2 oz) mushrooms in butter and place in the centre of the omelette before folding. Or grate 50 g (2 oz) cheese and mix half of it with the eggs before cooking. Sprinkle the remainder over the folded omelette before serving. Or skin and cut up a tomato. Fry lightly and place in the centre of the omelette before folding.

FISH - PYSGOD
STUFFED TROUT - BRITHYLL WEDI STWFFIO

METRIC	IMPERIAL
4 trout	*4 trout*
Stuffing	***Stuffing***
2 tablespoons cooked, shelled prawns	*2 tablespoons cooked, shelled prawns*
4 tablespoons breadcrumbs	*4 tablespoons breadcrumbs*
6 tablespoons dry white wine	*6 tablespoons dry white wine*
2 teaspoons mixed herbs	*2 teaspoons mixed herbs*
1 egg	*1 egg*
600 ml milk	*1 pint milk*
Sauce	***Sauce***
200 g button mushrooms	*8 oz button mushrooms*
50 g butter	*2 oz butter*
50 g flour	*2 oz flour*
salt and pepper	*salt and pepper*

Clean and gut the trout. Mix the prawns, breadcrumbs and herbs together. Season. Lightly beat the egg and use to bind the mixture. Place the stuffing in the fish. Put the fish in a buttered ovenproof dish and add the milk and wine. Bake in a moderate oven (180°C, 350°F, gas mark 4) for 15 minutes. Baste the fish occasionally with the wine liquor. **Sauce:** Slice the mushrooms and cook gently with half the butter. When cooked, remove the fish from the oven and decant off the liquor. Keep the fish warm. Melt the remaining butter in a saucepan and stir in the flour. Work to a smooth paste. Slowly stir in the fish liquor. Re-heat and boil gently for 2 - 3 minutes. Stir in the mushrooms and then pour over the fish.

POACHED TEIFI SALMON - EOG TEIFI WEDI'I BÔTSIO

METRIC	IMPERIAL
1 kg salmon steak	2 lb salmon steak
600 ml water	1 pint water
1 tablespoon lemon juice	1 tablespoon lemon juice
300 ml white wine	$\frac{1}{2}$ pint white wine
6 black peppercorns	6 black peppercorns
*1 bouquet garni	*1 bouquet garni

Place the fish in a fishkettle or large pan. Place all the other ingredients in a saucepan and warm to just below boiling. Pour over the fish and bring to the boil. Reduce the heat and keep just at simmering (the liquid should not boil) for 20 - 30 minutes until the flesh of the fish flakes easily. Carefully remove the fish. Skin and serve with buttered new potatoes, asparagus spears and Hollandaise sauce.(*Small muslin bag containing a sprig of thyme, a bay leaf, a sprig of parsley and a stick of celery.)

HOLLANDAISE SAUCE - SAWS HOLLANDAISE

METRIC	IMPERIAL
2 tablespoons wine vinegar	2 tablespoons wine vinegar
1 tablespoon water	1 tablespoon water
6 peppercorns, slightly crushed	6 peppercorns, slightly crushed
2 egg yolks	2 egg yolks
100 g unsalted butter	4 oz unsalted butter
salt and pepper	salt and pepper

Boil the wine vinegar, water and peppercorns until the volume has been reduced by half. Remove the peppercorns and leave to cool. Mix with the egg yolks and warm in a bowl standing over hot water. Whisk until the mixture is thick and fluffy. Gradually add the butter, a little at a time. Whisk after each addition. Season. If the sauce is too thick, add a few drops of lemon juice.

TROUT WITH ALMONDS - BRITHYLL GYDAG ALMONAU

METRIC
4 trout
2 tablespoons flour
salt and pepper
butter for frying
50 gm flaked almonds

IMPERIAL
4 trout
2 tablespoons flour
salt and pepper
butter for frying
2 oz flaked almonds

Clean and gut the trout. Season the flour and coat the fish with the flour. Melt a little butter in a frying pan and fry the fish until they are cooked and the flesh flakes easily. Remove the fish. Fry the almonds in a little fresh butter for 2 - 3 minutes. Sprinkle over the fish. Serve hot with wedges of lemon.

KIPPER PATÉ - PATÉ CIPER

METRIC
300 g kipper fillets
6 tablespoons dry white wine
2 tablespoons lemon juice
100 g butter
black pepper
1 tomato

IMPERIAL
12 oz kipper fillets
6 tablespoons dry white wine
2 tablespoons lemon juice
4 oz butter
black pepper
1 tomato

Remove the skin and any large bones from the fillets and place in the wine. Cover and leave to marinate in a cool place for 4 hours. Using a wooden spoon, work the fillets and marinade to a paste. Beat in the lemon juice. Warm the butter a little to soften it and beat into the fish mixture. Season with black pepper. Place in a 450 gm (1 lb) loaf tin and chill. To serve, turn out and decorate with slices of tomato. Serve with Melba toast.

SALMON COTTAGE CHEESE SALAD-
SALAD EOG A CHAWS BWTHYN

METRIC
200 g flaked cooked salmon
200 g cottage cheese
50 g chopped celery
50 g chopped sweet pickle
salad dressing
lettuce

IMPERIAL
8 oz flaked cooked salmon
8 oz cottage cheese
2 oz chopped celery
2 oz chopped sweet pickle
salad dressing
lettuce

Mix all the ingredients, except the lettuce together. Chill and serve on a bed of lettuce.

COCKLES - COCOS

METRIC
cockles
vinegar

IMPERIAL
cockles
vinegar

Scrub the cockles to remove sand and grit. Place in a saucepan of salted water and boil for 3 minutes. As soon as the shells open, remove from the heat and drain. Extract the cockles from the shells with a fork. Sprinkle with vinegar on a bed of lettuce in large shells and serve with thin brown bread and butter.

POACHED FISH WITH COCKLE SAUCE - PYSGODYN WEDI'I BÔTSIO GYDA SAWS COCOS

METRIC
450 g white fish
600 ml white wine and water mixed
1 tablespoon lemon juice
1 small carrot
1 stalk celery
6 black peppercorns

IMPERIAL
1 lb white fish
1 pint white wine and water mixed
1 tablespoon lemon juice
1 small carrot
1 stalk celery
6 black peppercorns

Peel and slice the carrot. Cut up the celery. Place the liquids, carrot, celery and peppercorns in a pan and heat until it is simmering. Add the fish and cover. Simmer gently allowing 10 - 15 minutes per 450 gm (1 lb) until the fish flakes easily. Remove the fish when cooked and used the strained liquid to make cockle sauce.

COCKLE SAUCE - SAWS COCOS

METRIC
4 tablespoons chopped cockles
25 g flour
25 g butter
2 teaspoons made up mustard
300 ml milk
300 ml water or 'fish liquor'

IMPERIAL
4 tablespoons chopped cockles
1 oz flour
1 oz butter
2 teaspoons made up mustard
½ pint milk
½ pint water or 'fish liquor'.

Prepare and cook the cockles as in the recipe for cockles on page 21. Chop coarsely. Melt the butter in a saucepan. Remove from the heat and add the flour. Work to a smooth paste. Stir in the milk, water and mustard. Heat gently for 2 - 3 minutes. Add the chopped cockles and reheat.

QUEEN SCALLOPS AND CHEESE SAUCE -
SGALOPS A SAWS CAWS

METRIC	IMPERIAL
4 scallops	*4 scallops*
1 tablespoon lemon juice	*1 tablespoon lemon juice*
50 g breadcrumbs	*2 oz breadcrumbs*
50 g grated cheese	*2 oz grated cheese*
15 g butter	*$\frac{1}{2}$ oz butter*
salt	*salt*
Sauce	***Sauce***
25 g butter	*1 oz butter*
25 g flour	*1 oz flour*
50 g grated cheese	*2 oz grated cheese*
300 ml milk	*$\frac{1}{2}$ pint milk*

Scrub the scallops and place in a moderate oven (170ºC, 325ºF, gas mark 3) until the shells open. Remove the brown part and gristly fibre leaving the red coral intact. Boil in salted water with the lemon juice for 10 minutes. Drain.
Sauce: Melt the butter in a saucepan. Remove from the heat and work in the flour to form a smooth paste. Stir in the milk and heat gently for 2 - 3 minutes. Stir in the cheese.
To serve: Clean the scalloped shells. Place a little sauce in each shell and sprinkle with breadcrumbs. Place a scallop in each shell, cover with more sauce and sprinkle with breadcrumbs and cheese. Dot with butter and bake at the top of a moderately hot oven (190ºC, 375ºF, gas mark 5) for 20 minutes. Garnish with parsley and serve with salad.

If the shells of the scallops are closed, they are fresh. If the shells are open, they should close immediately they are tapped. If they do not, the scallops are probably not fresh.

MEAT - CIGOEDD

LAMB PIES - PASTEIOD CIG OEN

METRIC
400 g lamb
100 g currants
100 g brown sugar
salt and pepper
Hot water pastry
400 g plain flour
100 g lard
200 ml water
pinch of salt

IMPERIAL
1 lb lamb
4 oz currants
4 oz brown sugar
salt and pepper
Hot water pastry
1 lb plain flour
4 oz lard
$\frac{1}{3}$ pint water
pinch of salt

Boil the lamb in salted water until tender. Drain, keeping the meat stock and removing any fat from the surface. Remove any bones and fat before mincing the meat.

Pastry: Sift the flour and salt together. Warm the water and melt the lard in it then bring to the boil. Make a well in the middle of the flour and pour the hot liquid into it. Work the liquid into the flour and knead to form a soft dough. Cover with a damp cloth and leave to rest for 30 minutes. Use two thirds of the pastry for the pastry cases and the remainder for the lids. Divide the pastry for the cases into six and roll each piece into a 15 cm (6 inch) round. Press each round over the base and up the sides of a 400 g (1 lb) jam jar. When cool, gently remove the jar. Fill the pastry cases with layers of lamb, currants and sugar. Moisten with a little meat stock. Season. Cover with pastry lids. Make a small hole in the top of each and cook in a moderate oven (180°C, 350°F, gas mark 4) for 1 hour. Warm the stock and fill the pies. Serve hot.

NEW YEAR PHEASANTS - FFESANTOD CALAN

METRIC

2 pheasants, jointed
25 g dripping
200 g swedes
200 g turnips
200 g parsnips
200 g carrots
200 g onions
25 g flour
4 tablespoons sherry
300 ml single cream
200 g tomatoes
salt and pepper
*bouquet garni

IMPERIAL

2 pheasants, jointed
1 oz dripping
8 oz swedes
8 oz turnips
8 oz parsnips
8 oz carrots
8 oz onions
1 oz flour
4 tablespoons sherry
$\frac{1}{2}$ pint single cream
8 oz tomatoes
salt and pepper
*bouquet garni

Fry the pheasants in the dripping. Remove the meat and place in a 2 litre (5 pint) ovenproof dish. Peel and dice the swedes, turnips, parsnips, carrots and onions. Fry and season. Drain and place the vegetables around the pheasant. Stir the flour into the fat in the pan. Mix the sherry and cream and add to the flour mixture. Heat gently for 5 minutes then pour over the pheasant. Add the tomatoes and bouquet garni and cook in a moderate oven (180ºC, 350ºF, gas mark 4) for 1 hour.

Bouquet garni: *Tie 1 small bay leaf, 6 peppercorns, 1 clove, 1 sprig of parsley, 1 sprig of thyme in a small muslin bag. Remove before serving.*

POTTED PORK - PORC MEWN POT

METRIC
400 g lean pork
100 g pork fat
150 g lamb's liver
6 rashers of streaky backon
2 onions
2 tablespoons brandy
1 tablespoon lemon juice
salt and pepper
1 teaspoon fresh sage
1 garlic clove, crushed (optional)

IMPERIAL
1 lb lean pork
4 oz pork fat
6 oz lamb's liver
6 rashers of streaky bacon
2 onions
2 tablespoons brandy
1 tablespoon lemon juice
salt and pepper
1 teaspoon fresh sage
1 garlic clove, crushed (optional)

Mince the pork and liver. Peel and mince the onions. Cut up the pork fat. Stretch the bacon rashers over the back of a knife. Line the bottom of a shallow bowl or terrine with 3 of the bacon rashers. Mix all the ingredients and season. Turn into the dish and place the remaining bacon rashers on top. Cover with foil or a lid and place the dish in a roasting tin half filled with water. Cook in a moderate oven (170ºC, 325ºF, gas mark 3) for 2 hours. Drain off the juices and keep. Place a piece of greaseproof paper on top of the cooked meat and then a weight. Leave in the refrigerator overnight. Remove any fat from the surface of the juices, warm the juices to liquefy them and pour over the meat. Leave to set in the refrigerator.

SPICED BEEF - CIG EIDION PERLYSIOG

METRIC

1 kg topside beef
300 ml water
3 tablespoons vinegar
2 small onions
50 g brown sugar
pinch mace
10 whole black peppers
1 teaspoon mixed pickling spices
300 ml red wine
3 teaspoons salt
1 tablespoon fat
200 g carrots
1 tablespoon flour

IMPERIAL

2 lb topside beef
$\frac{1}{2}$ pint water
3 tablespoons vinegar
2 small onions
2 oz brown sugar
pinch mace
10 whole black peppers
1 teaspoon mixed pickling spices
$\frac{1}{2}$ pint red wine
3 teaspoons salt
1 tablespoon fat
8 oz carrots
1 tablespoon flour

Skin and slice the onions. Mix the vinegar, water, onions, sugar, mace, peppers and spices together in a pan. Bring to the boil. Add the wine and pour the liquid over the meat. Leave in the refrigerator overnight. Next day, remove the meat from the liquid and rub the meat all over with salt. Place the meat with the fat in a pan and heat until the meat browns. Pour half the wine liquor over the meat. Cover and simmer for 1 hour. Peel and dice the carrots and add with the remaining liquor. Simmer for a further 1 hour. Remove from the heat and thicken the liquid in the pan with the flour. Reheat for 2- 3 minutes. Serve hot.

CHICKEN COBBLER - COBBLER FFOWLYN

METRIC
4 chicken breasts
25 g butter
100 g mushrooms
300 ml milk
150 ml water
1 teaspoon lemon juice
1 tablespoon flour
Topping
200 g plain flour
2 teaspoons baking powder
$\frac{1}{2}$ teaspoon mixed herbs
75 g butter
2 tablespoons milk

IMPERIAL
4 chicken breasts
1 oz butter
4 oz mushrooms
$\frac{1}{2}$ pint milk
$\frac{1}{4}$ pint water
1 teaspoon lemon juice
1 tablespoon flour
Topping
8 oz plain flour
2 teaspoons baking powder
$\frac{1}{2}$ teaspoon mixed herbs
3 oz butter
2 tablespoons milk

Fry the chicken and mushrooms in the butter for 5 minutes. Remove the mushrooms. Add the milk, water and lemon juice to the chicken. Cover and cook for 30 minutes. Thicken the liquid in the pan with the flour. Return the mushrooms and heat through for 2 - 3 minutes. Turn the chicken mixture into an ovenproof dish.

Topping: Sift the flour, baking powder and mixed herbs together. Rub the butter into the flour until the mixture looks like breadcrumbs. Mix with the milk to form a soft dough. Flatten the pastry to fit the dish and place on top of the chicken mixture. Mark with a criss-cross pattern using a knife. Cook in a hot oven (220°C, 425°F, gas mark 7) for 10 minutes until the topping is well risen and golden.

ROAST DUCK WITH ORANGE SAUCE -
HWYADEN RHOST A SAWS OREN

METRIC	IMPERIAL
1 duckling	*1 duckling*
salt	*salt*
1 orange	*1 orange*
1 tablespoon brandy	*1 tablespoon brandy*
watercress	*watercress*
Sauce	***Sauce***
3 oranges	*3 oranges*
1 lemon	*1 lemon*
1 teaspoon sugar	*1 teaspoon sugar*
1 tablespoon flour	*1 tablespoon flour*
300 ml water	*$\frac{1}{2}$ pint water*
3 tablespoons port wine	*3 tablespoons port wine*

Wipe the duck dry. Rub the skin with salt and prick all over with a fork to allow the fat beneath the skin to escape. Place the bird in a roasting tin. Cook in a moderately hot oven (200ºC, 400ºF, gas mark 6) for 15 minutes then reduce the heat (to 180ºC, 350ºF, gas mark 4) for 1½ - 2 hours until the duck is tender. Peel the rind from the orange and cut into very thin shreds. Simmer in hot water for 3 minutes. Drain and keep. Remove the pith from the orange and separate into segments. Sprinkle with brandy and leave to stand.

Sauce: Squeeze the juice from the 3 oranges and the lemon. Place 2 tablespoons of the liquor in the roasting tin in a saucepan. Add the sugar and heat until it is golden brown. Stir in the flour and cook for 2 - 3 minutes. Stir in the water and cook gently until the liquid thickens. Add the wine and orange juice. Season. Garnish the duck with orange segments and watercress and serve with orange sauce.

CHICKEN IN CIDER - FFOWLYN MEWN SEIDR

METRIC
4 chicken breasts
1 leek
Sauce
300 ml dry cider
50 g butter
1 large cooking apple
4 tablespoons single cream
salt and pepper

IMPERIAL
4 chicken breasts
1 leek
Sauce
½ pint dry cider
2 oz butter
1 large cooking apple
4 tablespoons single cream
salt and pepper

Soak the chicken in the cider for 2 hours. Remove the meat and keep the cider for the sauce. Trim the leek and cut into thin slices. Cover with cold water, heat and boil for 1 minute. Drain and cool immediately to keep its colour. Melt the butter in a thick based saucepan. Add the chicken breasts and cook for 5 minutes on each side. Peel and dice the apple. Add the apple and cider and cook for a further 10 minutes. Add the leeks and warm through. Season. Remove from the heat and stir in the cream.

CHICKEN AND CHEESE - FFOWLYN A CHAWS

METRIC
4 chicken breasts
50 g Welsh farmhouse cheese
25 g butter
1 tablespoon chopped parsley
4 rashers Welsh bacon
1 tablespoon lemon juice
mustard

IMPERIAL
4 chicken breasts
2 oz Welsh farmhouse cheese
1 oz butter
1 tablespoon chopped parsley
4 rashers Welsh bacon
1 tablespoon lemon juice
mustard

Cut a slit in each chicken breast. Fill with a slice of cheese seasoned with parsley and a little mustard. Wrap a bacon rasher around each piece of chicken and secure with a cocktail stick. Place the chicken in an ovenproof dish and bake in a moderately hot oven (200°C, 400°F, gas mark 6) for 20 minutes until the bacon is crisp and the chicken is cooked. Warm the butter in a saucepan and when it is hot, add the lemon juice. Pour over the chicken. Serve with jacket potatoes and green vegetables.

SNOWDONIA HOT POT - HOTPOT ERYRI

METRIC	IMPERIAL
200 g skinless pork sausages	8 oz skinless pork sausages
200 g lean ham	8 oz lean ham
200 g tomatoes	8 oz tomatoes
400 g potatoes	1 lb potatoes
1 apple	1 apple
1 onion	1 onion
2 tablespoons flour	2 tablespoons flour
1 teaspoon mixed herbs	1 teaspoon mixed herbs
salt and pepper	salt and pepper

Mix the flour, herbs and salt and pepper. Cut up the sausages and ham and dip in the seasoned flour. Slice the tomatoes. Peel and slice the potatoes, apple and onion. Arrange in layers in an ovenproof dish beginning with a layer of potatoes, then meat, then a mixture of apple, onion and tomato. Finish with a layer of potato. Season each layer lightly. Half fill the dish with water and cook in a moderate oven (180°C, 350°F, gas mark 4) for 2 hours.

GOWER PIE - PASTAI BRO GŴYR

METRIC

400 g stewing steak
200 g Gower potatoes
25 g butter
3 tablespoons milk
25 g beef dripping
1 large onion
1 tablespoon flour
salt and pepper

IMPERIAL

1 lb stewing steak
8 oz Gower potatoes
1 oz butter
3 tablespoons milk
1 oz beef dripping
1 large onion
1 tablespoon flour
salt and pepper

Remove as much fat as possible from the meat. Cut into pieces and mince. Peel the potatoes and boil in salted water. Drain, keeping the potato water. Mash with butter and milk. Skin and cut up the onion. Fry with the beef dripping until it is soft and beginning to brown. Remove from the heat and work in the flour. Add the potato water, stirring to prevent the formation of lumps. Add the meat, mix well and season. Simmer for 5 minutes. Turn the meat mixture into a buttered pie dish and cover with the mashed potatoes. Mark a pattern on the surface with a fork and cook in a hot oven (220°C, 425°F, gas mark 7) for 15 - 20 minutes until golden brown.

CAKES - TEISENNAU

HARVEST CAKE - CACEN CYNHAEAF

METRIC
Shortcrust pastry
200 g plain flour
100 g butter
3 tablespoons cold water
pinch salt
Filling
fruit in season
caster sugar

IMPERIAL
Shortcrust pastry
8 oz plain flour
4 oz butter
3 tablespoons cold water
pinch salt
Filling
fruit in season
caster sugar

The pastry: Sift the flour and salt together. Rub in the butter until the mixture looks like breadcrumbs. Add the water and form into a soft dough. Roll out half the pastry on a floured board and use to line a deep ovenproof dinner plate or flan dish.

Filling: Clean and prepare the fruit. Cover the pastry with the fruit. Add 1 tablespoon water and caster sugar to taste. Roll out the remaining pastry and cover the fruit. Brush the top with a little milk and sprinkle lightly with sugar. Bake in the centre of a fairly hot oven (220°C, 425°F, gas mark 7) for 20 minutes until the pastry is golden. Serve hot or cold with cream.

SHEARING CAKE - CACEN GNEIFIO

METRIC
400 g flour
1 teaspoon baking powder
200 g butter
300 g caster sugar
rind of 1 lemon
2 teaspoons caraway seeds
2 eggs
300 ml milk
pinch grated nutmeg

IMPERIAL
1 lb flour
1 teaspoon baking powder
8 oz butter
12 oz caster sugar
rind of 1 lemon
2 teaspoons caraway seeds
2 eggs
½ pint milk
pinch grated nutmeg

Sift the flour, baking powder and nutmeg together. Stir in the caraway seeds. Rub the butter into the flour mixture until it looks like breadcrumbs. Stir in the caster sugar. Beat the eggs. Stir the eggs and milk into the flour mixture. Turn into a baking tin lined with greased greaseproof paper and bake in a moderate oven (180°C, 350°F, gas mark 4) for 30 minutes then at 150°C, 300°F, gas mark 2 for a further 1½ hours.

THRESHING CAKE - CACEN DDYRNU

METRIC
400 g plain flour
1 teaspoon bicarbonate soda
400 g mixed dried fruit
200 g caster sugar

IMPERIAL
1 lb plain flour
1 teaspoon bicarbonate soda
1 lb mixed dried fruit
8 oz caster sugar

METRIC	IMPERIAL
*200 g butter	*8 oz butter
2 eggs	2 eggs
*1 tablespoon milk	*1 tablespoon milk

Rub the butter into the flour until the mixture looks like breadcrumbs. Stir in the sugar and dried fruit. Dissolve the bicarbonate of soda in a little milk. Lightly beat the eggs. Add the eggs and soda liquid to the cake mixture. Add enough milk to give a fairly soft consistency. Turn into a cake tin lined with greased greaseproof paper and bake in a moderately hot oven (200°C, 400°F, gas mark 6) for $1\frac{1}{2}$ hours.

Traditionally, bacon dripping and buttermilk were used.

TINKER'S CAKE - TEISEN DINCA

METRIC	IMPERIAL
400 g flour	1 lb flour
200 g butter	8 oz butter
150 g caster sugar	6 oz caster sugar
pinch salt	pinch salt
1 cooking apple	1 cooking apple

Sift the flour and salt together. Rub the butter into the flour until the mixture looks like breadcrumbs. Stir in the caster sugar. Peel and grate the apple. Add to the cake mixture and bind into a firm dough. Roll out and cut into rounds. Lightly grease a griddle or thick frying pan and warm to moderate heat. Bake until golden brown, turning to cook each side. Serve alone or buttered or with jam and cream.

LLANDDAROG FAIR CAKES - TEISENNAU FFAIR LLANDDAROG

METRIC
300 g self raising flour
200 g butter
150 g caster sugar
100 g mixed fruit
3 tablespoons beer

IMPERIAL
12 oz self raising flour
8 oz butter
6 oz caster sugar
4 oz mixed fruit
3 tablespoons beer

Rub the butter into the flour until the mixture looks like breadcrumbs. Stir in the sugar. Mix in the beer to form a soft dough. Roll out on a floured board to a thickness of 1.5 cm ($\frac{1}{2}$ inch). Cut into 5 cm (2 inch) rounds and press the fruit into the surface. Cook in a moderately hot oven (190ºC, 375ºF, gas mark 5) for 15 minutes.

OVERNIGHT CAKE - TEISEN DROS NOS

METRIC
200 g plain flour
100 g butter
100 g caster sugar
100 g dried mixed fruit
1 teaspoon cinnamon
1 teaspoon ground ginger
$\frac{1}{2}$ teaspoon bicarbonate of soda
1 tablespoon vinegar
2 tablespoons milk

IMPERIAL
8 oz plain flour
4 oz butter
4 oz caster sugar
4 oz dried mixed fruit
1 teaspoon cinnamon
1 teaspoon ground ginger
$\frac{1}{2}$ teaspoon bicarbonate of soda
1 tablespoon vinegar
2 tablespoons milk

Sift the flour and spices together. Rub the fat into the flour mixture until it looks like breadcrumbs. Stir in the sugar and dried mixed fruit. Add enough milk to give a fairly soft consistency. Dissolve the bicarbonate of soda in the vinegar and quickly stir into the cake mixture. Leave the batter to stand overnight. Next day pour the mixture into a cake tin lined with greased greaseproof paper and bake in a moderately hot oven (190ºC, 375ºF, gas mark 5) for 1 - 1¼ hours.

APPLE CAKE - DINCA FALA

METRIC
250 g self raising flour
125 g butter
125 g demerara sugar
400 g cooking apples
2 tablespoons milk

IMPERIAL
10 oz self raising flour
5 oz butter
5 oz demerara sugar
1 lb cooking apples
2 tablespoons milk

Rub the butter into the flour until the mixture looks like breadcrumbs. Stir in the sugar. Peel and dice the apples and add to the cake mixture. Add enough milk to make a fairly stiff dough. Flatten the dough and cook in a shallow greased cake tin in a moderately hot oven (190ºC, 375ºF, gas mark 5) for 30 minutes or until the cake is cooked.

ANGLESEY CAKE - CACEN SIR FÔN

METRIC

250 g self raising flour
100 g butter
75 g dark brown sugar
150 g dried mixed fruit
1 tablespoon black treacle
1 egg
1 teaspoon ground ginger
1 teaspoon mixed spice
½ teaspoon salt
½ teaspoon bicarbonate of soda
200 ml milk

IMPERIAL

10 oz self raising flour
4 oz butter
3 oz dark brown sugar
6 oz dried mixed fruit
1 tablespoon black treacle
1 egg
1 teaspoon ground ginger
1 teaspoon mixed spice
½ teaspoon salt
½ teaspoon bicarbonate of soda
⅓ pint milk

Cream the butter and sugar until light and fluffy. Beat in the egg and stir in the treacle. Sift the flour, ginger, spice and salt together and stir into the creamed mixture. Dissolve the bicarbonate of soda in the milk and stir into the cake mixture. Add the fruit and mix well. Turn into a 20 cm (8 inch) round cake tin lined with greased greaseproof paper and bake in a moderate oven (170ºC, 325ºF, gas mark 3) for 1 hour or until cooked.

CAERPHILLY SCONES - SGONAU CAERFFILI

METRIC
400 g self raising flour
75 g butter
75 g caster sugar
100 g Caerphilly cheese
300 ml milk
pinch salt

IMPERIAL
1 lb self raising flour
3 oz butter
3 oz caster sugar
4 oz Caerphilly cheese
$\frac{1}{2}$ pint milk
pinch salt

Sift the flour and salt together. Rub the butter into the flour until the mixture looks like breadcrumbs. Grate the cheese and stir with the sugar into the flour mixture. Add the milk slowly until a soft, firm dough is formed. Turn on to a floured board and roll out to a thickness of 5 cm (2 inches). Cut into rounds and brush with milk. Cook on a greased baking tray in a hot oven (220°C, 425°F, gas mark 7) for 10 minutes. Serve hot and buttered.

BARDSEY ISLAND CAKES - CACENNAU YNYS ENLLI

METRIC
150 g self raising flour
100 g butter
50 g caster sugar

IMPERIAL
6 oz self raising flour
4 oz butter
2 oz caster sugar

Melt the butter in a warmed basin and beat in the sugar. Gradually add the flour, mixing well with a warm spoon. Roll out thinly on a floured board and cut into rounds. Cook in a moderately hot oven (190°C, 375°F, gas mark 5) for 15 minutes or until golden. Serve sprinkled with sugar and sandwiched with whipped cream and strawberry jam.

DESSERTS - PWDINAU

SNOWDON PUDDING - PWDIN ERYRI

METRIC	IMPERIAL
100 g suet	*4 oz suet*
3 eggs	*3 eggs*
25 g cornflour or ground rice	*1 oz cornflour or ground rice*
75 g demerara sugar	*3 oz demerara sugar*
100 g breadcrumbs	*4 oz breadcrumbs*
50 g stoned raisins	*2 oz stoned raisins*
75 g lemon marmalade	*3 oz lemon marmalade*
1 lemon	*1 lemon*
pinch salt	*pinch salt*

Mix the suet, breadcrumbs, cornflour and salt together. Grate the rind of the lemon and add with the sugar. Grease the inside of a pudding basin and press half the raisins on to the greased surface. Beat the eggs with the marmalade and add with the remaining raisins to the suet mixture. Pour into the basin. Cover and boil for $1\frac{1}{2}$ hours. Serve hot.

TREACLE TART - TARTEN DRIOG

METRIC	IMPERIAL
Pastry	**Pastry**
100 g plain flour	*4 oz plain flour*
pinch salt	*pinch salt*
50 g butter	*2 oz butter*

Filling
200 g golden syrup
50 g breadcrumbs
2 lemons

Filling
8 oz golden syrup
2 oz breadcrumbs
2 lemons

Pastry: Sift the flour and salt together. Rub fat into the flour until the mixture looks like breadcrumbs. Add enough water to form a firm dough. Roll out on a floured board and line a 18 cm (7 inch) ovenproof flan dish.

Filling: Grate the rind of the lemons. Mix the syrup, breadcrumbs, lemon rind and 2 teaspoons lemon juice together. Pour into the pastry case. Roll out any pastry pieces left over and cut into strips. Lay across the tart. Bake in a moderately hot oven (190°C, 375°F, gas mark 5) for 25 minutes until the pastry is cooked.

ORANGE SHORTBREAD - TEISENNAU 'BERFFRO OREN

METRIC
100 g plain flour
50 g cornflour
100 g butter
50 g caster sugar
1 orange

IMPERIAL
4 oz plain flour
2 oz cornflour
4 oz butter
2 oz caster sugar
1 orange

Cream the butter and caster sugar together. Grate the rind of the orange and add to the creamed mixture. Sift the flour and cornflour together and add a little at a time to the mixture. Place the shortbread on a baking sheet and roll out to a 20 cm (8 inch) circle. Pinch the edges with a fork and prick all over. Cut into 12 sections. Sprinkle with caster sugar. Leave to cool in a refrigerator for 15 minutes. Bake in a moderate oven (170°C, 325°F, gas mark 3) for 35 minutes. Place on a wire tray to cool.

MONMOUTH PUDDING - PWDIN MYNWY

METRIC
150 g breadcrumbs
25 g sugar
25 g butter
3 egg yolks
450 ml milk
1 lemon
4 tablespoons raspberry jam
Topping
3 egg whites
75 g caster sugar

IMPERIAL
6 oz breadcrumbs
1 oz sugar
1 oz butter
3 egg yolks
¾ pint milk
1 lemon
4 tablespoons raspberry jam
Topping
3 egg whites
3 oz caster sugar

Grate the rind of the lemon. Add the lemon rind, sugar and butter to the milk and bring to the boil. Pour over the breadcrumbs and leave to stand for 15 minutes. Stir the egg yolks into the cool pudding mixture. Warm the jam. Pour half the pudding mixture into a greased ovenproof dish and spread with half the jam. Add the remainder of the pudding and cover with the rest of the jam. Bake in a moderate oven (170°C, 325°F, gas mark 3) for 40 - 45 minutes.

Topping: Beat the egg whites until stiff and fold in the caster sugar using a metal spoon. Cover the pudding with the meringue and bake in a cool oven (150°C, 300°F, gas mark 2) for 20 minutes until the meringue is lightly browned.

WELSH PANCAKES -
CREMPOG CYMREIG (FFROIS CYMREIG)

METRIC	**IMPERIAL**
100 g plain flour	*4 oz plain flour*
pinch salt	*pinch salt*
1 egg	*1 egg*
300 ml milk and water	*½ pint milk and water*
fat for frying	*fat for frying*

Sift the flour and salt together. Make a well in the centre of the flour and add the egg. Add 2 tablespoons of the liquid and mix well together, making sure that there are no lumps. Gradually add the remaining liquid, beating well after each addition and keeping the batter smooth and free from lumps. Leave to stand for 30 minutes. Beat again. Heat a little fat in a thick based frying pan until it is quite hot. Pour enough batter into the pan to just cover the base. Tilt the pan to ensure the batter spreads evenly. When cooked on one side, turn and cook the other side. Turn on to a warm plate. Sprinkle the pancake with sugar and roll up. Serve hot with lemon.

APPLE PANCAKES - CREMPOG AFAL

Prepare pancake batter as in the above recipe. Warm peeled, chopped cooking apples with a little butter, brown sugar and brandy to taste. Pile in the centre of the cooked pancakes and roll up. Sprinkle with brown sugar and a little cinnamon (optional). Serve warm with whipped cream.

STRAWBERRY PANCAKES - CREMPOG MEFUS

Prepare pancake batter as in the above recipe. Wash and hull the strawberries. Pile in the centre of the cooked pancakes, sprinkle with caster sugar and roll up. Serve warm with whipped cream.

PRESERVES AND JAMS - CYFFAITH A JAM

APPLE CHUTNEY - SHWTNI AFAL

METRIC
1 kg cooking apples
1 kg onions
300 g sultanas
400 g demerara sugar
2 lemons
450 ml malt vinegar

IMPERIAL
2 lb cooking apples
2 lb onions
12 oz sultanas
1 lb demerara sugar
2 lemons
¾ pint malt vinegar

Peel, core and dice the apples. Skin and cut up the onions. Place the apples, onions and sultanas in a pan. Grate the lemon rind and squeeze and strain the juice. Add the rind, juice, sugar and vinegar to the pan. Bring to the boil and simmer until the mixture thickens with no excess liquid. Pot in sterilized jars and cover.

TOMATO CHUTNEY - SHWTNI TOMATO

METRIC
2 kg tomatoes
2 tablespoons mustard seed
1 tablespoon whole allspice
1 teaspoon cayenne pepper
250 g sugar
4 teaspoons salt
450 ml white vinegar

IMPERIAL
4 lb tomatoes
2 tablespoons mustard seed
1 tablespoon whole allspice
1 teaspoon cayenne pepper
8 oz sugar
4 teaspoons salt
¾ pint white vinegar

Immerse the tomatoes in boiling water for 1 - 2 minutes then in cold water. The skins will now peel off easily. Place the skinned tomatoes in a pan. Tie the mustard seed and allspice in a muslin bag and add with the cayenne pepper to the tomatoes. Simmer for 45 minutes until the mixture is reduced to a pulp. Add the sugar, salt and vinegar. Continue simmering until the mixture thickens with no excess liquid. Pot in sterilized jars and cover.

STRAWBERRY CONSERVE - CYFFAITH MEFUS

METRIC	IMPERIAL
2 kg strawberries	*4 lb strawberries*
2 kg sugar	*4 lb sugar*

Hull and wash the strawberries. Place the whole fruit in a large dish covering each layer with sugar. Leave for 24 hours. Turn into a pan and heat. Bring to the boil, stirring until the sugar dissolves. Boil rapidly for 5 minutes. Return the mixture to the dish and leave for a further 48 hours. Again, place in the pan and boil rapidly until setting point is reached. Cool and pot in sterilized jars and cover. (To test for a set: Place a small teaspoonful of the preserve on a cold saucer, cool for 20 seconds then run a finger through it. If the preserve wrinkles at the edges and stays in two separate sections, it is ready.)

BLACKBERRY AND APPLE JAM - JAM MWYAR AC AFAL

METRIC	IMPERIAL
2 kg blackberries	*4 lb blackberries*
700 gm apples, peeled, cored and diced	*1 lb apples, peeled, cored and diced*
2.5 kg sugar	*6 lb sugar*
300 ml water	*½ pint water*

Wash the blackberries and place in a pan with 150 ml (¼ pint) water. Simmer until the fruit is soft. Simmer the diced apples with the remaining water and mash them with a fork. Add the blackberries and sugar. Bring to the boil and boil rapidly, stirring frequently until the setting point is reached. Pot in sterilized jars and cover. (To test for a set see the recipe for strawberry conserve.)

CONFECTIONERY - MELYSFWYD

COCONUT ICE - BARRAU COCONYT

METRIC
450 g granulated sugar
150 ml milk
150 g desiccated coconut
pink colouring

IMPERIAL
1 lb granulated sugar
$\frac{1}{4}$ pint milk
5 oz desiccated coconut
pink colouring

Warm the milk with the sugar until the sugar dissolves. Bring to the boil and simmer for about 10 minutes until the soft ball stage is reached (116°C, 240°F). Remove from the heat and stir in the coconut. Pour half the mixture quickly into a greased 15 cm (6 inch) square tin. Colour the second half of the mixture and pour over the first. Leave until nearly set. Mark into bars and cut or break up when cold. **Soft ball stage:** When a drop of the fondant is put into very cold water, it forms a soft ball. The soft ball flattens on being removed from the water and the higher the temperature, the firmer the ball.

HONEYCOMB TOFFEE - TAFFI TYLLOG

METRIC
450 g granulated sugar
300 ml water
4 tablespoons vinegar
$\frac{1}{2}$ teaspoon bicarbonate of soda

IMPERIAL
1 lb granulated sugar
$\frac{1}{2}$ pint water
4 tablespoons vinegar
$\frac{1}{2}$ teaspoon bicarbonate of soda

Heat the water, sugar and vinegar together until the sugar dissolves. Bring to the boil and boil gently to soft crack stage (141°C, 285°F). Remove the heat and add the bicarbonate of soda to the toffee. Stir thoroughly and pour into a greased 18 cm (7 inch) square tin. Leave until half set. Mark into squares and leave to set. **Soft crack stage:** When a drop of the toffee is placed in cold water, the syrup separates into threads which are hard but not brittle.

INDEX - MYNEGAI

INDEX - MYNEGAI continued